Christmas '91
Dan Smolich

The Bathroom Sports Quote Book

THOUGHTS
FROM THE THRONE—
WIT AND WISDOM
FROM THE WORLD
OF SPORTS

The Bathroom Library™

Introduction

THE BATHROOM SPORTS QUOTE BOOK was conceived during the fifth annual movement of National Bathroom Reading Week. (Honest. There really is such an event— the second week of May every year.) It is in keeping with this sit-down observance that this book is presented.

You, the bathroom-reading sports fan, will be afforded quick relief with wit and wisdom about the games people play. Inside, you'll find hundreds of quips and quotes from front office figures (*Branch Rickey:* "Luck is the residue of design") to the just plain funny (*Yogi Berra:* "I didn't say everything I said I did").

Well documented is the fact that the average person will spend seven years of his or her life in the bathroom. I fervently hope that this lavatory literature will help you to put some of that valuable time to good use.

Yours flushingly,

Jack Kreismer
Publisher

The Bathroom Sports Quote Book

By

Jack Kreismer

RED-LETTER PRESS, INC.
SADDLE RIVER, NEW JERSEY

Champions take responsibility. When the ball is coming over the net, you can be sure I want the ball.

—*Billie Jean King*

* * * *

Don't forget to miss it.

—*Dizzie Dean*

* * * *

Baseball is like church. Many attend. Few understand.

—*Leo Durocher*

* * * *

If I had my way, any man guilty of golf would be ineligible for any office of trust in the United States.

—*H.L. Mencken*

* * * *

A true sports fan is one who can leave a game and ask, "What cheerleaders?"

—*Al Batt*

Thoughts of the Throne
(Tommy) Lasorda's standard reply when some new kid would ask directions to the whirlpool was to tell him to stick his foot in the toilet and flush it.

—*Steve Garvey*

---

* * * *

There's nothing better in life than a head-on collision.

—*Lawrence Taylor*

* * * *

They wanted an arm and a leg.

—*Martina Navratilova, on why she never insured her left arm with Lloyds of London*

* * * *

It's a game in which you can feel a clean hatred for your opponent.

—*Ronald Reagan, on football*

When I was a small boy in Kansas, a friend of mine and I went fishing, and as we sat there in the warmth of a summer afternoon on a riverbank, we talked about what we wanted to do when we grew up. I told him that I wanted to be a real major league baseball player, a genuine professional like Honus Wagner. My friend said that he'd like to be President of the United States. Neither of us got our wish.

—*President Dwight D. Eisenhower*

* * * *

Nobody roots for Goliath.   —*Wilt Chamberlain*

* * * *

I always turn to the sports pages first, which record people's accomplishments. The front page has nothing but man's failures.   —*Chief Justice Earl Warren*

* * * *

It's what you learn after you know it all that counts.

—*John Wooden*

Baseball is the most intellectual game because most of the action goes on in your head. —*Henry Kissinger*

* * * *

I'm waiting for the day we see the 'wave' at the Metropolitan Opera. —*Al Michaels*

* * * *

The man who complains about the way the ball bounces is likely the one who dropped it. —*Lou Holtz*

* * * *

It's a mere moment in a man's life between an All-Star Game and an Old-Timer's Game. —*Vin Scully*

* * * *

I quit school in the fifth grade because of pneumonia. Not because I had it but because I couldn't spell it. —*Rocky Graziano*

Beware the big play: the 80-yard drive is better than the 80-yard pass.
—*Fran Tarkenton*

* * * *

He's a perfectionist. If he was married to Racquel Welch, he'd expect her to cook.
—*Don Meredith, on Tom Landry*

* * * *

The most...perfect expression of national stupidity.
—*Max Beerbohm, on golf*

* * * *

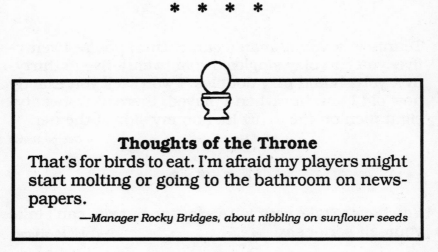

Thoughts of the Throne
That's for birds to eat. I'm afraid my players might start molting or going to the bathroom on newspapers.
—*Manager Rocky Bridges, about nibbling on sunflower seeds*

The greatest name in football.

—*Alex Karras, on Browns wide receiver Fair Hooker*

* * * *

Catching a fly ball is a pleasure, but knowing what to do with it is a business.

—*Tommy Henrich*

* * * *

I got bald.

—*Alex Hannum, when asked why his height is now 6 feet 7 but in his basketball playing days it was listed at 6 feet 8*

* * * *

Tennis is a young man's game. Until you're twenty-five, you can play singles. From twenty-five to thirty-five, you should play doubles. I won't tell you exactly how old I am, but when I played, there were twenty-eight men on the court just on my side of the net.

—*George Burns*

* * * *

You have to take your job seriously, but you can't take yourself seriously.

—*Brent Musburger*

If my quarterback runs, I'll shoot him.

—Bill Parcells, on the New York Giants run and shoot offense

* * * *

A complete ballplayer today is one who can hit, field, run, throw and pick the right agent.

—San Francisco Giants owner Robert Lurie

* * * *

I find it to be the hole in one.

—Groucho Marx, when asked about golf's toughest shot

* * * *

A team is where a boy can prove courage on his own. A gang is where a coward goes to hide.

—Mickey Mantle

* * * *

There are three types of people ... People who make things happen. People who watch things happen. And people who don't know what's happening.

—John Madden

The most beautiful thing in the world is a ballpark filled with people. —*Bill Veeck*

* * * *

I probably couldn't play for me. I wouldn't like my attitude. —*Georgetown basketball coach John Thompson*

* * * *

A good sport has to lose to prove it. —*Anonymous*

* * * *

Take it easy and lazily, because the golf ball isn't going to run away from you while you're swinging. —*Sam Snead*

* * * *

I knew it was time to quit when I was chewing out an official and he walked off the penalty faster than I could keep up with him. —*Chicago Bears coach George Halas*

Lay off for a few weeks and then quit for good.
—*Sam Snead, to a golf student*

* * * *

A school without football is in danger of deteriorating into a medieval study hall. —*Vince Lombardi*

* * * *

On the day of the race, a lot of people want you to sign something just before you get in the car so that they can say they got your last autograph.
—*Racecar driver A.J. Foyt*

* * * *

The key is not the "will to win" ... everybody has that. It is the will to *prepare* to win that is important.
—*Bobby Knight*

* * * *

Skiing combines outdoor fun with knocking down trees with your face. —*Dave Barry*

I'm playing like Tarzan- and scoring like Jane.
—*Golfer Chi Chi Rodriguez*

* * * *

Sports do not build character. They reveal it.
—*Heywood Hale Broun*

* * * *

I believe that professional wrestling is clean and everything else in the world is fixed. —*Frank Deford*

* * * *

I went to the fights the other night and a hockey game broke out. —*Rodney Dangerfield*

* * * *

Ninety percent of the putts that fall short don't go in.
—*Yogi Berra*

When you're playing for the national championship, it's not a matter of life or death. It's more important than that.
—*Duffy Daugherty*

* * * *

You wonder how they do it and you look to
   see the knack,
You watch the foot in action, or the shoulder,
   or the back,
But when you spot the answer where the
   higher glamours lurk,
You'll find in moving higher up the
   laurel covered spire,
That most of it is practice and the
   rest of it is work.
—*Grantland Rice*

* * * *

If I just had some humility, I'd be perfect.   —*Ted Turner*

* * * *

Trade a player a year too early rather than a year too late.
—*Branch Rickey*

19

Boxing can be summed up in one word ... You never know.
—*Fight manager Lou Duva*

* * * *

If Shakespeare had been in pro basketball, he never would have had time to write his soliloquies. He would have always been on a plane between Phoenix and Kansas City.
—*Basketball coach Paul Westhead*

* * * *

Thoughts of the Throne

In Kansas City, I had a phone in my bathroom. In the minors, I stayed in hotels where the fire escape was a rope.
—*Boston Red Sox coach Tony Torchia, on life in the minor leagues*

* * * *

I'm not concerned with your liking or disliking me... All I ask is that you respect me as a human being.
—*Jackie Robinson*

The best part of playing for the Indians is that you don't have road trips to Cleveland.

—*Ken "Hawk" Harrelson*

* * * *

It's a very interesting game. They have big bears up front and little rabbits in the back. The idea is for the bears to protect the rabbits.

—*Soviet hockey coach Viktor Tikonov, on the sport of football*

* * * *

I don't trust doctors. They are like golfers. Every one has a different answer to your problem.

—*Seve Ballesteros*

* * * *

My wife wanted a big diamond.

—*Mookie Wilson, on why he was married in a ballpark*

* * * *

Some people who don't say ain't, ain't eating.

—*Dizzy Dean*

Pro football gave me a good sense of perspective when I entered the political arena. I had already been booed, cheered, cut, sold, traded, and hanged in effigy.

—*Jack Kemp*

* * * *

All that running and exercise can do for you is make you healthy.

—*Denny McLain*

* * * *

It's just a job. Grass grows, birds fly, waves pound the sand. I beat people up.

—*Muhammad Ali*

* * * *

It isn't really the stars that are expensive. It's the high cost of mediocrity.

—*Bill Veeck*

* * * *

Prayer never seems to work for me on the golf course. I think it has something to do with my being a terrible putter.

—*Reverend Billy Graham*

Now there's three things you can do in a baseball game; you can win or you can lose or it can rain.

—*Casey Stengel*

* * * *

Nothing is as good as it used to be, and it never was. The "golden age of sports," the golden age of anything, is the age of everyone's childhood. —*Ken Dryden*

* * * *

The taste of defeat has a richness of experience all its own. —*Bill Bradley*

* * * *

Cool Papa Bell was so fast he could get out of bed, turn out the lights across the room, and be back in bed under the covers before the lights went out.

—*Josh Gibson*

* * * *

Show me a good loser and I'll show you a loser.

—*Anonymous*

It's like watching Mario Andretti park a car.
—*Ralph Kiner, describing Phil Niekro's knuckleball*

*   *   *   *

We have 51 golf courses in Palm Springs. He never decides which course he will play until after his first tee shot.   —*Bob Hope, about former President Gerald Ford*

*   *   *   *

Hitting is better than sex.   —*Reggie Jackson*

*   *   *   *

Build up your weaknesses and they become your strong points.   —*Knute Rockne*

*   *   *   *

The difference between hitting .300 and .270 is a hit and a half a week.
—*Chicago Cubs first baseman Mark Grace*

They're taking over the game. They've got locker rooms, draft choices, and everything. Mary Sue there probably went in the first round. Good hands.

—John Madden, on cheerleaders

* * * *

What I really hate about umpiring is that we can never win. We don't walk off a field with a grin on our faces.

—Ron Luciano

* * * *

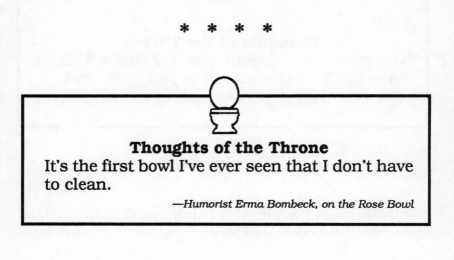

Thoughts of the Throne
It's the first bowl I've ever seen that I don't have to clean.

—Humorist Erma Bombeck, on the Rose Bowl

* * * *

Why are we honoring this man? Have we run out of human beings?
—Milton Berle, at a Howard Cosell roast

Opera in English is, in the main, just about as sensible as baseball in Italian.
—*H.L. Mencken*

* * * *

Be quick, but never hurry.
—*John Wooden*

* * * *

Thoughts of the Throne
The thing I like about football is that you don't have to take a shower before you go to work.
—*Chicago Bears center Jay Hilgenberg*

* * * *

I know a lot of people who think I'm dumb. Well, at least I ain't no educated fool.
—*Leon Spinks*

* * * *

Say this for big league baseball - it is beyond any question the greatest conversation piece ever invented in America.
—*Bruce Catton*

Quick guys get tired. Big guys don't shrink.
—*Marv Harshman, University of Washington basketball coach,*
on why he prefers size rather than speed

* * * *

Always go to other people's funerals, otherwise they won't come to yours. —*Yogi Berra*

* * * *

Never have so many spent so much to sit in relative comfort to brag about their failures.
—*Keith Jackson, on golfers*

* * * *

Look like a woman, but play like a man.
—*Jan Stephenson*

* * * *

If hockey fights were fixed, I'd be in more of them.
—*Rod Gilbert*

I deny allegations by Bob Hope that during my last game (of golf) I hit an eagle, a birdie, an elk, and a moose.
—*Gerald Ford*

* * * *

Jogging is very beneficial. It's good for your legs and your feet. It's also very good for the ground. It makes it feel needed.
—*Snoopy*

* * * *

If all the year were playing holidays,
To sport would be as tedious as to work.
—*Shakespeare*

* * * *

It is committee meetings, called huddles, separated by outbursts of violence.
—*George Will, on football*

Every obnoxious fan has a wife home who dominates him.
—*Al McGuire*

* * * *

Sweat plus sacrifice equals success.
—*Charlie Finley*

* * * *

The game is my wife. It demands loyalty and responsibility, and it gives me back fulfillment and peace.
—*Michael Jordan*

* * * *

A waist is a terrible thing to mind.
—*Overweight Atlanta Braves pitcher Terry Forster*

* * * *

You gotta be a man to play baseball, but you gotta have a lot of little boy in you, too.
—*Roy Campanella*

It's still embarrassing. I asked my caddie for a sand wedge, and ten minutes later he came back with a ham on rye.

—*Chi Chi Rodriguez, talking about his accent*

* * * *

Thoughts of the Throne

It always did look like a toilet bowl. Now it has a seat on it.

—*Whitey Herzog,
about the new roof on Olympic Stadium in Montreal*

* * * *

Saltwater taffy.

—*Caldwell Jones, former Portland Trail Blazer center,
naming his favorite seafood*

* * * *

But I signed a contract, and I pitch for what I signed for. Think about it - your signature on a contract is the same as your word.

—*Nolan Ryan, explaining why he wound up with a pay cut*

I'm a ballplayer, not an actor.

—Joe DiMaggio, on why, even after a home run,
he maintained a serious look

* * * *

Statistics are used by baseball fans in much the same way that a drunk leans against a street lamp; it's there more for support than for enlightenment.

—Vin Scully

* * * *

When you're winning, you don't need any friends. When you're losing, you don't have any friends anyway.

—Woody Hayes

* * * *

I clashed with the drapes.

—Jake LaMotta, former middleweight boxing champ,
on why his wife left him

* * * *

You know what NFL stands for? Not For Long.

—Jerry Glanville, on coaching in the National Football League

31

I once thought about playing football but you have to wear too much equipment and people can't see you.

—*Muhammad Ali*

*　*　*　*

Thoughts of the Throne

His hands got so dirty that he used to wash them *before* he went to the men's room.

—*Columnist Mike Royko,*
about Chicago Cubs third baseman Ron Santo

*　*　*　*

I never had a bad night in my life, but I've had a few bad mornings.

—*Hall of Fame pitcher Lefty Gomez*

*　*　*　*

The important thing is to learn a lesson every time you lose.

—*John McEnroe*

The trick is growing up without growing old.

—*Casey Stengel*

* * * *

Kill the body and the head will die.   —*Joe Frazier*

* * * *

I have a lifetime contract. That means I can't be fired during the third quarter if we're ahead and moving the ball.

—*Lou Holtz*

* * * *

Good pitching always stops good hitting and vice versa.

—*Bob Veale*

* * * *

Winning can be defined as the science of being totally prepared.

—*George Allen*

Serious sport has nothing to do with fair play. It is bound up with hatred, jealousy, boastfulness, disregard of all rules and sadistic pleasure in witnessing violence: in other words it is war minus the shooting.

—*George Orwell*

* * * *

If Howard Cosell was a sport, it would be roller derby.

—*Jimmy Cannon*

* * * *

I have only one superstition. I make sure to touch all the bases when I hit a home run.   —*Babe Ruth*

* * * *

I consider playing basketball...the most shallow thing in the world.   —*Bill Russell*

34

If you make every game a life-and-death proposition, you're going to have problems. For one thing, you'll be dead a lot.
—*Dean Smith*

* * * *

The more we lose, the more he'll fly in. And the more he flies in, the better the chance there'll be a plane crash.
—*Graig Nettles, on New York Yankees owner George Steinbrenner*

* * * *

If Borg's parents hadn't liked the name, he might never have been Bjorn.
—*Marty Indik*

* * * *

No comment.
—*Doug Moe, responding to his having been voted the most quotable coach in the NBA*

It matters not the sacrifice
Which makes the duffer's wife so sore.
I am the captive of my slice
I am the servant of my score.

—*Grantland Rice*

* * * *

The only difference between me and General Custer is
that I have to watch films on Sunday.

—*Rick Venturi, Northwestern football coach*

* * * *

Thoughts of the Throne
He must shower in vaseline.

—*Lester Hayes, L.A. Raiders cornerback,
on the elusiveness of Philadelphia Eagles quarterback
Randall Cunningham*

* * * *

Tackling is more natural than blocking. If a man is
running down the street with everything you own, you
won't let him get away. That's tackling.

—*Vince Lombardi*

36

Ninety feet between home plate and first base may be the closest man has ever come to perfection.

—Red Smith

* * * *

My family was so poor they couldn't afford any kids. The lady next door had me.

—Lee Trevino

* * * *

I don't like the idea of practicing six days to play one.

—Baseball player Robin Yount, on the game of football

* * * *

When we played softball, I'd steal second, then feel guilty and go back.

—Woody Allen

* * * *

Baseball is a game played by idiots for morons.

—F. Scott Fitzgerald

Everybody wants to go to heaven, but nobody wants to die.

—*Joe Louis*

* * * *

He who have the fastest cart never have to play bad lie.

—*Mickey Mantle, on golf*

* * * *

San Francisco has always been my favorite booing city. I don't mean the people boo louder or longer, but there is a very special intimacy. When they boo you, you know they mean you. Music, that's what it is to me. One time in Kezar Stadium they gave me a standing boo.

—*Chicago Bears coach George Halas*

* * * *

The highlight of my baseball career came in Philadelphia's Connie Mack Stadium when I saw a fan fall out of the upper deck. When he got up and walked away the crowd booed.

—*Bob Uecker*

If you aren't fired with enthusiasm, you'll be fired with enthusiasm.
—Vince Lombardi

* * * *

Tennis is a perfect combination of violent action taking place in an atmosphere of total tranquility.
—Billie Jean King

* * * *

As I understand it, sport is hard work for which you do not get paid.
—Irvin S. Cobb

* * * *

Luck is the residue of design.
—Branch Rickey

* * * *

It's not the size of the dog in the fight, but the size of the fight in the dog.
—Diminutive running back Archie Griffin, on winning two Heisman Trophies

All pro athletes are bilingual. They speak English and profanity.

—*Gordie Howe*

* * * *

Some people are so busy learning the tricks of the trade that they never learn the trade.

—*Pittsburgh Pirates pitcher
Vernon Law*

* * * *

College football today is one of the last great strong-holds of genuine old-fashioned American hypocrisy.

—*Paul Gallico*

* * * *

As a nation we are dedicated to keeping physically fit-and parking as close to the stadium as possible.

—*Bill Vaughn*

* * * *

I just try to concentrate on concentrating.

—*Martina Navratilova*

If you've got to remind yourself to concentrate during competition, you've got no chance to concentrate.

—*Golfer Bobby Nichols*

* * * *

One loss is good for the soul. Too many losses are not good for the coach.

—*Knute Rockne*

* * * *

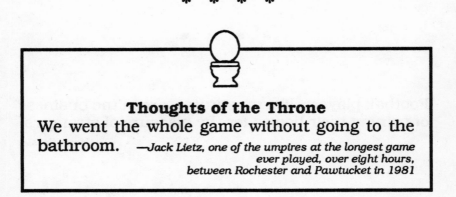

Thoughts of the Throne

We went the whole game without going to the bathroom. —*Jack Lietz, one of the umpires at the longest game ever played, over eight hours, between Rochester and Pawtucket in 1981*

* * * *

Nolan Ryan is pitching much better now that he has his curve ball straightened out.

—*Joe Garagiola*

* * * *

It matters not whether you win or lose; what matters is whether I win or lose.

—*Darrin Weinberg*

If you don't have a hero, you'll never be disillusioned.
—*Derek Sanderson*

* * * *

A player's got to be kept hungry to become a big leaguer. That's why no boy from a rich family ever made the big leagues.
—*Joe DiMaggio*

* * * *

Football players, like prostitutes, are in the business of ruining their bodies for the pleasure of strangers.
—*Merle Kessler*

* * * *

Publicity is like poison: it doesn't hurt unless you swallow it.
—*Joe Paterno*

* * * *

When you're as great as I am, it's hard to be humble.
—*Muhammad Ali*

Baseball is almost the only orderly thing in a very unorderly world. If you get three strikes, even the best lawyer in the world can't get you off.　　—*Bill Veeck*

* * * *

If God had intended man for racing, He would have given him four legs like a horse.　　—*Red Smith*

* * * *

If it is true that a sports career prolongs adolescence, it is also true that when that career ends, it deposits a player into premature middle age.　　—*Ken Dryden*

* * * *

Everybody's negotiable.　　—*Muhammad Ali*

* * * *

Baseball is what we were, football is what we've become.　　—*Mary McGrory*

Forecheck, backcheck, paycheck.
—Gil Perreault, Buffalo Sabres center,
on the three most important elements of pro hockey

* * * *

If you spend a lot of time on sportsmanship, you're going to spend a lot of time losing.
—Tulsa football coach Glen Dobbs

* * * *

Everything is 60-40 against.
—Satchel Paige

* * * *

Tennis is like marrying for money. Love has nothing to do with it.
—Phyllis Diller

* * * *

I seldom refused autograph seekers, unless they were old enough to look like collection agents.
—Joe Pepitone

44

Thoughts of the Throne

It seems to me the official rule book should be called the funny pages. It obviously doesn't mean anything. The rule book is only good for you when you go deer hunting and run out of toilet paper.

—*Billy Martin, after particularly frequent run-ins with the umpires*

Jerry Ford is a nice guy, but he played too much football with his helmet off. —*Lyndon B. Johnson*

* * * *

I found out that it's not good to talk about my troubles. Eighty percent of the people who hear them don't care and the other twenty percent are glad you're having trouble. —*Tommy Lasorda*

* * * *

When I was little, I was big. —*William "Refrigerator" Perry*

The injuries are brutal and the fields stink; at the end of the game they smell of vomit and spit and blood because it doesn't go into the earth. All the odors just cook there on this plastic turf.

—*Writer Norman Mailer, on football fields made of artificial surfaces*

* * * *

Golf and sex are about the only things you can enjoy without being good at.

—*Jimmy Demaret*

* * * *

Thoughts of the Throne
County Stadium in Milwaukee has the busiest urinals I've ever seen. People are so drunk that they keep 'em on automatic flush.

—*Anonymous*

* * * *

We Americans are a peculiar people. We are for the underdog no matter how much of a dog he is.

—*Onetime baseball commissioner A.B. "Happy" Chandler*

Umpiring is best described as the profession of standing between two seven-year-olds with one ice cream cone.
—*Ron Luciano*

* * * *

For when the One Great Scorer comes to mark against
    your name,
He writes— not that you won or lost— but how you
    played the Game.
—*Grantland Rice*

* * * *

Grantland Rice, the great sportswriter, once said, "It's not whether you win or lose, it's how you played the game." Well, Grantland Rice can go to hell as far as I'm concerned.
—*California Angels owner Gene Autry*

* * * *

A team should be an extension of the coach's personality. My teams were arrogant and obnoxious.
—*Former basketball coach Al McGuire*

I have tried terribly to like Howard (Cosell), and I have failed miserably.
—*Red Smith*

* * * *

Gary Player is all right if you like to see a grown man dressed up like Black Bart all the time.
—*Don Rickles*

* * * *

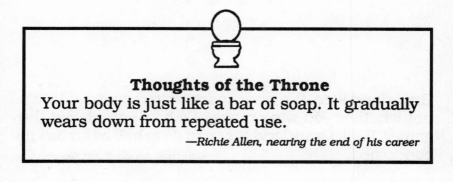

Thoughts of the Throne
Your body is just like a bar of soap. It gradually wears down from repeated use.
—*Richie Allen, nearing the end of his career*

* * * *

I tackle everybody and then throw them away until I come to the one with the ball.
—*Former defensive lineman Gene "Big Daddy" Lipscomb*

Throw high risers at the chin; throw peas at the knees; throw it here when they're lookin' there; throw it there when they're lookin' here. —*Satchel Paige*

* * * *

Anyone who will tear down sports will tear down America. Sports and religion have made America what it is today. —*Woody Hayes*

* * * *

First your legs go. Then you lose your reflexes. Then you lose your friends. —*Boxer Willie Pep*

* * * *

If you can react the same way to winning and losing, that...quality is important because it stays with you the rest of your life. —*Chris Evert*

* * * *

There's no pressure playing baseball....Pressure is when you have to go to the unemployment office to pick up a check to support four people.

—*George Brett*

He's turned his life around. He used to be depressed
and miserable. Now he's miserable and depressed.

—Announcer Harry Kalas,
about Philadelphia Phillies center fielder Garry Maddox

*　*　*　*

Thoughts of the Throne

Horses and jockeys mature earlier than people—
which is why horses are admitted to race tracks
at the age of two, and jockeys before they are old
enough to shave. *—Dick Beddoes*

*　*　*　*

If you see a defensive team with dirt and mud on their
backs they've had a bad day. *—John Madden*

*　*　*　*

Blind people come to the park just to listen to him
pitch. *—Reggie Jackson, on Tom Seaver*

This record is going to be hard to break.
—TCU wide receiver James Maness,
after catching a 99 yard touchdown pass

* * * *

Putting a fighter in the business world is like putting silk stockings on a pig. *—Boxing manager Jack Hurley*

* * * *

I don't think we can win every game. Just the next one.
—Lou Holtz

* * * *

Oldtimers' weekends and airplane landings are alike. If you can walk away from them, they're successful.
—Casey Stengel

* * * *

It's a lot tougher to be a football coach than a president. You've got four years as president, and they guard you. A coach doesn't have anyone to protect him when things go wrong. *—Harry S Truman*

51

For the parent of a Little Leaguer, a baseball game is simply a nervous breakdown divided into innings.

—*Earl Wilson*

* * * *

I'm playing military golf- left, right, left, right, left, right...

—*Golfer Bob Menne, on his inconsistency in hitting drives down the middle of the fairway*

* * * *

If there's one pitch you keep swinging at and keep missing, stop swinging at it.

—*Yogi Berra*

* * * *

If God had meant Wimbledon to be played in great weather, he would have put it in Acapulco.

—*Anonymous*

Sport begets tumultuous strife and wrath, and wrath begets fierce quarrels and war to the death.

—*Horace*

*   *   *   *

A golf course is the epitome of all that is transitory in the universe, a space not to dwell in, but to get over as quickly as possible. —*Jean Giraudoux*

*   *   *   *

To see some of our best-educated boys spending the afternoon knocking each other down, while thousands cheer them on, hardly gives a picture of a peace-loving nation. —*Lyndon Baines Johnson, on football*

*   *   *   *

Becoming number one is easier than remaining number one. —*Bill Bradley*

Kids should practice autographing baseballs. This is a skill that's often overlooked in Little League.

—*Tug McGraw*

* * * *

You really never lose until you stop trying.   —*Mike Ditka*

* * * *

Boxing is a great sport and a dirty business.

—*Ken Norton*

* * * *

The Good Lord was good to me. He gave me a strong body, a good right arm and a weak mind.   —*Dizzy Dean*

* * * *

You never get ahead of anyone as long as you try to get even with him.

—*Lou Holtz*

The more violent the body contact of the sports you watch, the lower your class. —*Paul Fussell*

* * * *

Fear of losing is what makes competitors so great. Show me a gracious loser and I'll show you a permanent loser. —*O. J. Simpson*

* * * *

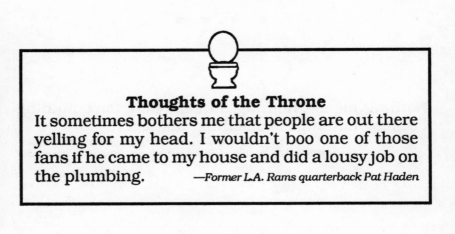

Thoughts of the Throne
It sometimes bothers me that people are out there yelling for my head. I wouldn't boo one of those fans if he came to my house and did a lousy job on the plumbing. —*Former L.A. Rams quarterback Pat Haden*

* * * *

Games played with the ball, and others of that nature, are too violent for the body and stamp no character on the mind. —*Thomas Jefferson*

Have you ever noticed what golf spells backwards?

—*Al Boliska*

* * * *

Horses are like strawberries; you must enjoy them while you can, because they don't last long.

—*Charlie Whittingham, trainer*

* * * *

Nothing means nothing, but it really isn't nothing because nothing is something that isn't.

—*Darryl Dawkins, Philadelphia 76ers center,*
announcing that he would no longer be speaking with the media

* * * *

Arrogant, pompous, obnoxious, vain, rude, persecuting, distasteful, verbose, a show-off. I have been called all of these. Of course, I am. —*Howard Cosell*

I always wanted to be a player, but I never had the talent to make the big leagues. So I did the next best thing: I bought a team. —*Charlie Finley*

* * * *

It's almost like life. Just when it begins to look rosy, somebody will intercept a pass and run ninety yards against you. —*Former NFL Films narrator John Facenda, on football*

* * * *

Mike Anderson's limitations are limitless.
—*Danny Ozark, Philadelphia Phillies manager,*
on his outfielder's ability

* * * *

I never met a man I didn't want to fight. —*Lyle Alzado*

* * * *

The key to winning baseball games is pitching, fundamentals and three-run homers. —*Earl Weaver*

If I ever needed a brain transplant, I'd choose a sportswriter because I'd want a brain that had never been used.
—*Norm Van Brocklin*

* * * *

I never cease to amaze myself. I say this humbly.
—*Don King*

* * * *

I'm very even-tempered on the golf course. I stay mad all the time.
—*Bob Murphy*

* * * *

Basketball is like war in that offensive weapons are developed first, and it always takes awhile for the defense to catch up.
—*Red Auerbach*

* * * *

Baseball is ninety percent mental. The other half is physical.
—*Yogi Berra*

Once when I was golfing in Georgia I hooked the ball into the swamp. I went in after it and found an alligator wearing a shirt with a picture of a little golfer on it.   —*Buddy Hackett*

* * * *

If you're lucky enough to find a guy with a lot of head and a lot of heart, he'll never come off the field second.
                                                        —*Vince Lombardi*

* * * *

Be good or begone.   —*Bear Bryant*

* * * *

Almost the only place in life where a sacrifice is really appreciated.   —*Mark Beltaire, on baseball*

* * * *

Middle age is when you start for home about the same time you used to start for somewhere else.
                                        —*Boxing promoter Chris Dundee*

I just use my muscles as a conversation piece, like someone walking a cheetah down 42nd Street.

—*Arnold Schwarzenegger*

* * * *

Because even the Good Lord has trouble hitting a one-iron.

—*Lee Trevino, who once was struck by lightning, explaining why he holds his one-iron over his head when there's a storm on the golf course*

* * * *

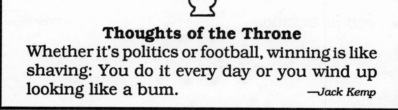

Thoughts of the Throne
Whether it's politics or football, winning is like shaving: You do it every day or you wind up looking like a bum.

—*Jack Kemp*

* * * *

A winner never whines.

—*Paul Brown*

* * * *

The real superstar is a man or a woman raising six kids on $150 a week.

—*Spencer Haywood*

Our players don't do dances in the end zone. We like them to act like they've been there before.

—*Lou Holtz, at the time the coach of the Arkansas Razorbacks*

*   *   *   *

I never heard of Gehrig until I came here. And I always thought Babe Ruth was a cartoon character. I really did.

—*Don Mattingly*

*   *   *   *

The way to make coaches think you're in shape in the spring is to get a tan.

—*Whitey Ford*

*   *   *   *

I never made the team... I was not heavy enough to play the line, not fast enough to play halfback, and not smart enough to be a quarterback.

—*Richard M. Nixon*

I hate all sports as rabidly as a person who likes sports hates common sense. —*H.L. Mencken*

* * * *

Hurting people is my business. —*Sugar Ray Robinson*

* * * *

You don't do things right once in a while. You do them right all the time. —*Vince Lombardi*

* * * *

A little bit of perfume doesn't hurt you if you don't drink it. —*Texas football coach Darrell Royal*

* * * *

Baseball is very big with my people. It figures. It's the only time we can get to shake a bat at a white man without starting a riot. —*Dick Gregory*

No, I clean giraffe ears.
—*Elvin Hayes, six foot nine former Washington Bullets forward, when someone asked him if he was a basketball player*

* * * *

How can you think and hit at the same time?
—*Yogi Berra*

* * * *

They should move first base back a step to eliminate all the close plays.
—*John Lowenstein*

* * * *

Thoughts of the Throne
The wind was so strong there were whitecaps in the porta-john.
—*Joyce Kazmierski, on network television at the 1983 Women's Kemper Open golf tournament, talking about weather conditions*

* * * *

People always ask me if success is going to change me, and I tell them I sure hope so.
—*Randall "Tex" Cobb, former heavyweight fighter*

Football is not a contact sport. It's a collision sport. Dancing is a good example of a contact sport.

—*Duffy Daugherty*

* * * *

In America it is sport that is the opiate of the masses.

—*Russell Baker*

* * * *

Golf is an awkward set of bodily contortions designed to produce a graceful result.
—*Tommy Armour*

* * * *

Hating the Yankees is as American as pizza pie, unwed mothers and cheating on your income tax.

—*Mike Royko*

* * * *

I learned that you cannot be taught anything by anyone but yourself.

—*Jean-Claude Killy, when asked about his education as a skier*

Our game plan is first year, a .500 season. Second year, a conference championship. Third year, undefeated. Fourth, a national championship. And by the fifth year, we'll be on probation, of course.

—*Alabama coach Bear Bryant*

* * * *

Sometimes they write what I say and not what I mean.

—*Pedro Guerrero, on sportswriters*

* * * *

Nothing improves a fisherman's luck like fish in a biting mood. —*Catfish Moore*

* * * *

Trying to sneak a pitch past Hank Aaron is like trying to sneak the sunrise past a rooster. —*Joe Adcock*

When you win, nothing hurts. —*Joe Namath*

* * * *

Thoughts of the Throne
Even the men's room has a double dogleg.
—*Dave Stockton, complaining of the difficulty of playing
Poppy Hills Golf Course in Pebble Beach, California*

* * * *

I never graduated from Iowa but I was only there for two terms — Truman's and Eisenhower's. —*Alex Karras*

* * * *

If you can't beat 'em in the alley, you can't beat 'em on the ice. —*Connie Smythe*

The Superbowl is our great national campfire around which we cluster. —*George Will*

* * * *

I'd give up golf if I didn't have so many sweaters. —*Bob Hope*

* * * *

Putting lights in Wrigley Field is like putting aluminum siding on the Sistine Chapel. —*Columnist Roger Simon*

* * * *

Thoughts of the Throne

We've got a problem. Luis Tiant wants to use the bathroom and it says no foreign objects in the toilet.

—*Graig Nettles, during a New York Yankees' airplane trip*

Golf does strange things to other people, too. It makes liars out of honest men, cheats out of altruists, cowards out of brave men and fools out of everybody.

—*Milton Gross*

* * * *

Your Holiness, I'm Joseph Medwick. I, too, used to be a Cardinal.

—*Joseph "Ducky" Medwick, a former St. Louis Cardinal outfielder. During a World War II visit to the Vatican, the above quote was his response to the Pope asking about his vocation.*

* * * *

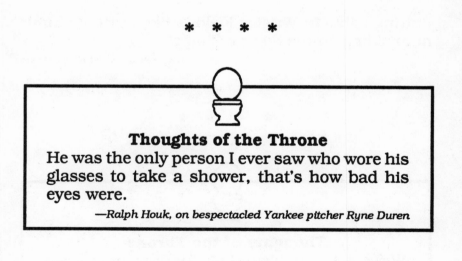

Thoughts of the Throne

He was the only person I ever saw who wore his glasses to take a shower, that's how bad his eyes were.

—*Ralph Houk, on bespectacled Yankee pitcher Ryne Duren*

* * * *

Thinking...is what gets you caught from behind.

—*O.J. Simpson*

A life isn't significant except for its impact on other lives.
— *Jackie Robinson*

* * * *

Statistics always remind me of the fellow who drowned in a river whose average depth was only three feet.
— *Woody Hayes*

* * * *

Yeah, Will Rogers.
— *Joe Don Looney, Washington Redskin running back, when asked if he ever met a man he didn't like*

* * * *

Thoughts of the Throne
Once I tried to drown myself with a shower nozzle after I gave up a homer in the ninth. I found out you can't.
— *Kansas City Royals relief pitcher Dan Quisenberry*

Win any way you can as long as you can get away with it.

—*Leo Durocher*

* * * *

It is impossible to imagine Goethe or Beethoven being good at billiards or golf.

—*H.L. Mencken*

* * * *

My toughest fight was with my first wife.

—*Muhammad Ali*

* * * *

If you don't get it by midnight, chances are you ain't gonna get it; and if you do, it ain't worth it.

—*Casey Stengel*

* * * *

In golf you're always breaking a barrier. When you bust it, you set yourself a little higher barrier, and try to break that one.

—*Jack Nicklaus*

My theory is that if you buy an ice-cream cone and make it hit your mouth, you can play. If you stick it on your forehead, your chances are less.

—*Vic Braden, tennis instructor*

* * * *

He was the best man in our fights, too.

—*Jake LaMotta, talking about the best man at his wedding, Sugar Ray Robinson*

* * * *

Al is inquisitive, knowledgeable, and incredibly well prepared. I don't know what his IQ is, but it's probably only a couple of points lower than mine.

—*Dan Dierdorf, on Monday Night Football broadcasting partner Al Michaels*

* * * *

Baseball is a ballet without music. Drama without words. A carnival without kewpie dolls.

—*Broadcaster Ernie Harwell*

71

When a man wants to murder a tiger he calls it sport; when a tiger wants to murder him he calls it ferocity.

—*George Bernard Shaw*

*   *   *   *

Being a sports fan is a complex matter, in part irrational...but not unworthy ... a relief from the seriousness of the real world, with its unending pressures and often grave obligations.   —*Richard Gilman*

*   *   *   *

Baseball gives you every chance to be great. Then it puts every pressure on you to prove that you haven't got what it takes. It never takes away the chance, and it never eases up on the pressure.   —*Joe Garagiola*

*   *   *   *

You must have an alibi to show why you lost. If you haven't one, you must fake one. Your self-confidence must be maintained.   —*Christy Mathewson*

Thoughts of the Throne

When you've got two broken hands with casts on 'em and you go to the men's room, that's where you really find out who your friends are.

—CBS-TV broadcaster Alex Hawkins, when Miami defensive back Jake Scott entered the game with two broken hands

If you don't throw it, they can't hit it.   *—Lefty Gomez*

* * * *

You may glory in a team triumphant, but fall in love with a team in defeat.   *—Roger Kahn*

* * * *

Ronald Reagan has held the two most demeaning jobs in the country — President of the United States and radio broadcaster of the Chicago Cubs.   *—George Will*

* * * *

Some players you pat their butts, some players you kick their butts, some players you leave alone.

—Pete Rose

Some coaches pray for wisdom. I pray for 260-pound tackles.
—*Wake Forest football coach Chuck Mills*

* * * *

If a man watches three football games in a row, he should be declared legally dead.
—*Erma Bombeck*

* * * *

The only thing duller than track is field.
—*Texas University publicist Jones Ramsay*

* * * *

Ball handling and dribbling are my strongest weaknesses.
—*David Thompson*

* * * *

If you think it's hard to meet new people, try picking up the wrong golf ball.
—*Jack Lemmon*

74

The larger the ball, the less the writing about the sport. There are superb books about golf, very good books about baseball, not many good books about football, and very few good books about basketball. There are no books about beachballs. —*George Plimpton*

* * * *

How you play the game is for college boys. When you're playing for money, winning is the only thing that matters. —*Leo Durocher*

* * * *

Thoughts of the Throne

We are not surgeons, or even plumbers. Society cannot do without those skills; it can certainly do without ballplayers. —*Steve Garvey*

* * * *

A racetrack is a place where windows clean people. —*Comedian Danny Thomas*

The qualities and capacities that are important in running- such factors as will power, the ability to apply effort during extreme fatigue and the acceptance of pain have a radiating power that subtly influences one's life.   —*Jim Fixx*

* * * *

They give you a round bat, and they throw a round ball, and they tell you to hit it square.   —*Willie Stargell*

* * * *

A catcher and his body are like an outlaw and his horse: You've got to ride that nag 'til it drops.
—*Johnny Bench*

* * * *

There have been only two geniuses in the world - Willie Mays and Willie Shakespeare.   —*Tallulah Bankhead*

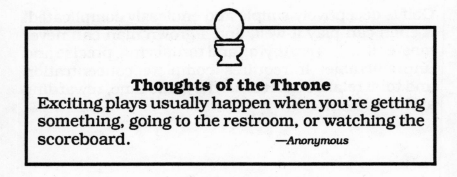

Thoughts of the Throne

Exciting plays usually happen when you're getting something, going to the restroom, or watching the scoreboard.

—*Anonymous*

There weren't many alleys that would let me come back. I have an overhand delivery.

—*Actor John Wayne, on why he gave up bowling*

* * * *

Before you can win a game, you have to not lose it.

—*Chuck Noll*

* * * *

As I remember it, the bases were loaded.

—*Garry Maddox, when asked to describe a grand slam homer he'd hit*

* * * *

He had a God-given killer instinct.

—*Raiders owner Al Davis, on quarterback George Blanda*

Golf is deceptively simple and endlessly complicated. A child can play it well, and a grown man can never master it....It is gratifying and tantalizing, precise and unpredictable; it requires complete concentration and total relaxation. It is, at the same time, rewarding and maddening.

—*Arnold Palmer*

* * * *

The problem is that when you get it, you're too damned old to do anything about it.

—*Jimmy Connors, on experience*

* * * *

Sports is like a war without the killing.

—*Ted Turner*

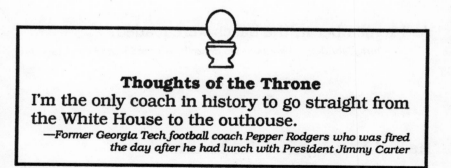

Thoughts of the Throne
I'm the only coach in history to go straight from the White House to the outhouse.

—*Former Georgia Tech football coach Pepper Rodgers who was fired the day after he had lunch with President Jimmy Carter*

Basketball can serve as a kind of metaphor for ultimate cooperation. It is a sport where success, as symbolized by the championship, requires that the dictates of community prevail over selfish personal impulses.
—*Bill Bradley*

* * * *

Thoughts of the Throne
I had done all the work around the house, and my wife gave me two options - clean the toilets or clean behind the refrigerator. I thought it was time for me to get back to work.
—*Atlanta Falcons guard R.C. Thielemann,
on why he ended his five-week holdout*

Officiating is the only occupation in the world where the highest accolade is silence.
—*NBA referee Earl Strom*

* * * *

I have to get that hit this year. I might die.
—*Pittsburgh Pirates outfielder Roberto Clemente, on his 3,000th hit.
Clemente finished the 1972 season with exactly 3,000 career hits. On
December 31, 1972, he was killed in a plane crash.*

My father is an undertaker, and I worked for him part-time. There were certain advantages to the job. For instance, while I was dating my wife I sent her flowers every day.
—Notre Dame basketball coach Digger Phelps,
explaining how he was nicknamed

* * * *

A second-guesser is one who don't know anything about the first guess, and he's one who needs two guesses to get one right.
—Tommy Lasorda

* * * *

Golf is a lot like taxes. You drive hard to get to the green and then wind up in the hole.
—Anonymous

* * * *

Thoughts of the Throne
He's a guy paid to talk while everyone else goes to the bathroom.
—Sportscaster Bill Currie,
explaining the job of the color man on a broadcast

Playing baseball for a living is like having a license to steal.
—*Pete Rose*

* * * *

He (my father) really believed in discipline. So did my mother. Till I was thirteen, I thought my name was "Shut Up."
—*Joe Namath*

* * * *

"Angling" is the name given to fishing by people who can't fish.
—*Stephen Leacock*

* * * *

We'll do all right if we can capitalize on our mistakes.
—*Former Texas Rangers outfielder Mickey Rivers*

81

The difference between a successful person and others is not a lack of strength, not a lack of knowledge, but lack of will.

—*Vince Lombardi*

* * * *

Quit coaching? I'd croak in a week.

—*Alabama coach Bear Bryant*
(He retired following a Liberty Bowl victory on December 26, 1982, and died of a heart attack January 26, 1983.)

* * * *

What has happened is that all your life you operated businesses in such a way that you could one day afford to buy a baseball team. And then you buy the team and forget all the business practices that enabled you to buy it.

—*Bill Veeck, on New York Yankees owner George Steinbrenner*

* * * *

Thoughts of the Throne
I flush the john between innings to keep my wrists strong.

—*Baltimore Orioles designated hitter John Lowenstein, on how he stays ready while on the bench*

There is still nothing in life as constant and as changing at the same time as an afternoon at a ballpark.
—*TV and radio personality Larry King*

* * * *

It's not whether you win or lose, but who gets the blame.
—*Former Dallas Cowboys lineman Blaine Nye*

* * * *

Just once I'd like to see the win-loss records of doctors right out front where people could see them - won ten, lost three, tied two.
—*Texas basketball coach Abe Lemons*

* * * *

All of the Mets' road wins against Los Angeles this year have been at Dodger Stadium.
—*New York Mets broadcaster Ralph Kiner*

* * * *

Every ball park used to be unique. Now it's like women's breasts - if you've seen one, you've seen both.
—*Former pitcher Jim Kaat*

If the people don't want to come out to the park, nobody's gonna stop them.

—*Yogi Berra*

* * * *

I prefer fast food.

—*Rocky Bridges, San Francisco Giants coach, explaining why he won't eat snails*

* * * *

I prefer rugby to soccer. When soccer players start biting each other's ears off again, maybe I'll like it better.

—*Actress Elizabeth Taylor*

* * * *

Thoughts of the Throne
I stayed at the club last year and my room was so clean, I didn't even want to take a shower.

—*Lee Trevino, on the Riviera Golf Club, Pacific Palisades, California*

They can make 250 bats from one good tree. How's that for a statistic, baseball fans? —*Andy Rooney*

* * * *

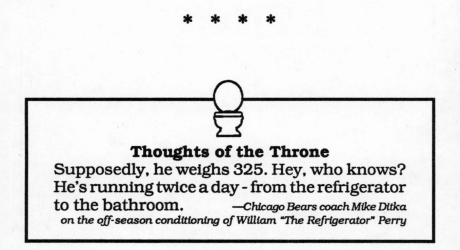

Thoughts of the Throne
Supposedly, he weighs 325. Hey, who knows? He's running twice a day - from the refrigerator to the bathroom. —*Chicago Bears coach Mike Ditka*
on the off-season conditioning of William "The Refrigerator" Perry

* * * *

Never argue with people who buy ink by the gallon.
—*Tommy Lasorda, on the press*

Thoughts From The Throne

Write your own Bathroom Inspired Gems on these pages:

Thoughts From The Throne

Write your own Bathroom Inspired Gems on these pages:

Thoughts From The Throne

Write your own Bathroom Inspired Gems on these pages:

Thoughts From The Throne

Write your own Bathroom Inspired Gems on these pages:

Thoughts From The Throne

Write your own Bathroom Inspired Gems on these pages:

Thoughts From The Throne

Write your own Bathroom Inspired Gems on these pages:

Thoughts From The Throne

Write your own Bathroom Inspired Gems on these pages:

Thoughts From The Throne

Write your own Bathroom Inspired Gems on these pages:

Thoughts From The Throne

Write your own Bathroom Inspired Gems on these pages:

Thoughts From The Throne

Write your own Bathroom Inspired Gems on these pages:

The
Bathroom Library

THE BATHROOM BASKETBALL BOOK
THE BATHROOM GUEST BOOK
THE BATHROOM CROSSWORD PUZZLE BOOK
THE BATHROOM DIGEST
THE BATHROOM TRIVIA BOOK
THE BATHROOM ENTERTAINMENT BOOK
THE BATHROOM SPORTS QUIZ BOOK
THE BATHROOM SPORTS QUOTE BOOK
THE BATHROOM GAME BOOK
THE BATHROOM BASEBALL BOOK
THE BATHROOM FOOTBALL BOOK
THE BATHROOM GOLF BOOK
THE BATHROOM SOAP OPERA BOOK
THE BATHROOM INSPIRATION BOOK

For further information, write to:
Red-Letter Press, Inc.
P.O. Box 393,
Saddle River, N.J. 07458